D1830402

A PRIMER OF MALAYALAM LITERATURE

A PRIMER
OF
MALAYALAM LITERATURE

T. K. KRISHNA MENON

GYAN

Published by

Gyan Publishing House
5, Ansari Road
Daryaganj, New Delhi-110002
Phone: 011-47034999, 9811692060
E-mail: books@gyanbooks.com

Distribution Network
gyanbooks.com
India, USA, Canada, UK, Australia, France

ISBN : 978-81-212-3029-2 (PB)
First Published, 1939

2nd Impression 2020

Printed at: Gyan Press, Delhi.

A Primer of Malayalam Literature
Author: T. K. Krishna Menon

A PRIMER
OF
MALAYALAM LITERATURE

INTRODUCTION

I am desired by the author of this Primer to introduce him to his readers, and I have much pleasure in complying with his kind and agreeable request. Mr. T. K. Krishna Menon is sufficiently well known to his countrymen, with whose national literature he deals in the following pages. He comes of a respectable Nayar family of Cochin which produced two Prime Ministers for that State. He has made a name for himself. He is one of the few graduates of the Madras University who, in obedience to the solemn oath they are required to take on receiving their degrees, have endeavoured to diffuse their light and learning among their less fortunate countrymen. It was he who got Mr. R. C. Dutt's *Ancient India* translated into Malayalam. As a former Editor of the best Malayalam Magazine, the *Vidya Vinodini*, he has done invaluable service to periodical literature. He has had the rare fortune of associating in wedlock with an English educated partner in life. The young lady, T. C. Kalyani Amma, his worthy consort, has started a useful series named *Books for Malabar Bairns*, which appear under the able editorship of her talented husband, and is editing, along with others, a Ladies' Magazine called the *Sarada*. In fact, this philanthropic couple is always at something or other to carry the torch of light into the benighted homes of the masses.

As drawn by so qualified a gentleman, the short sketch is sure to commend itself to those who take any interest in the literary advancement of the Malayalees. An article on the same theme has already appeared from the able pen of Mr. Menon in a recent issue of the *Journal of the Royal Asiatic Society* of which he is a worthy member. The present paper goes deeper into the subject and is also much more descriptive. This too, however, gives only a bird's eye view of the subject as the author himself confesses. As such it does not enter into any detailed criticism of style or characteristics of the authors it deals with. Yet it does not fail to touch upon the important points, and contains in its short compass a concise account of the literary history of a cultured community. This much I can say with a fair amount of certainty, that a lay reader will hardly miss in the following pages any information he may wish to have concerning Malayalam literature.

KERALA VARMA
(Valiya Koil Tampuran).

1897.

AUTHOR'S NOTE

I wrote this brochure, while a college student, at the instance of the late Mr. R. C. Dutt, who wanted it for a work called the *History of Hindu Civilization under British Rule* which his son-in-law, the late Mr. P. N. Bose, Head of the Geological Department, was then writing. In this I have now made only such changes as the lapse of time necessitated. I am glad to say that this has received the benefit of the revision of His Highness the late Valiya Koil Tampuran, C.S.I., of his nephew, the late Mr. A. R. Rajaraja Varma, M.A., then Professor of Sanskrit and Malayalam in the Maharaja's College at Trivandrum, of my revered master, the late Mr. D. M. Cruickshank, M.A., who was the Director of Public Instruction in the Cochin State, and of my friend Professor P. Sankaran Nambiar, M.A., himself a scholar and poet and the author of a short history of Malayalam literature. Professor Rajaraja Varma then wrote to me, " I am reading your manuscript again and again. No flaw as yet met my scrutinising eye. It is a tiny, elegant compendium on Malayalam literature. If published as it is, the pamphlet will be a great boon to the candidates of the B.A. Degree Examination." The index was prepared by my young friend, Mr. P. Parameswaran Moothathu, B.A., B.L. To all these gentlemen I am indebted to a high degree.

It was my eldest sister who first taught me Sanskrit, in which she was well versed, My other two sisters too were learned in that, the youngest more than her elders. It was the elder sister who has left her mark in the history of Malayalam literature by her drama *Subhadrarjunam*. My eldest sister used to teach her sisters and cousins Sanskrit. Similarly, my wife's grandmother spent her lifetime in giving free tuition in Sanskrit to those who went to her for that. And they were many. She was a profound Sanskrit scholar, and learnt logic under the author of *Gadadhariyam*. The late Valiya Koil Tampuran, after once hearing her *vakyarthapratipadana*, was so pleased with it that he composed three complimentary *slokams* about her.

This humble offering is intended for these four lady scholars.

15th April 1939.
Ernakulam,
Kumārālayam

T. K. KRISHNA MENON.

CONTENTS

OPINIONS

" Malabar Mail" writes:—The author needs no introduction to the Malayalam readers. His services in the field of literature and other allied subjects are so widely appreciated. This short work, written while he was a College student but modified as the lapse of time necessitated, gives a sketch of the origin and growth of the Malayalam literature. He begins with an account of the country where Malayalam is spoken, and scientifically deals with the origin of the language. Then the various epochs in the history of the literature is narrated, i.e. period of (1) Karintamil 3100—100 B. C. (2) of Old Malayalam 100 B.C.—325 A. D. (3) of Middle Malayalam 325 A. D.—1425 A. D. and (4) of Modern Malayalam from 1425 A. D. The learned author, while giving a brief account of these various periods, makes reference to the leading literary works and their authors. The latter portion of the book which deals with modern Malayalam is sufficiently descriptive, so that the readers will get a clear idea of the growth and developments of our literature in its full vigour.

It is regrettable that even most of our educated people are lacking in the knowledge of the history of our literature. One important reason for this sad situation is the absence of suitable works. These landmarks, coming from the pen of such an eminent scholar as Mr. Krishna Menon, will be highly appreciated not only by Malayalees but also by those who attempt to have some idea of the origin and growth of the Malayalam literature.

Rao Sahib Mahakavi Ullur S. Parameswara Aiyar, M. A., B. L. thus writes about it : " This brief account of the Malayalan Language and Literature, which Sahityakusalan T. K. Krishna Menon has appended as a supplementary Note to the fourth volume of the *History of Kerala,* edited by him, is a work of inestimable value. As a general introduction to the study of the literature of Kerala I cannot think of a better book. It deals with all the phases of the literary history of Kerala in a lucid, logical, correct and concise manner, explains present day tendencies and developments, and exhibits the several influences to which the authors of Kerala have reacted from time to time."

Rao Bahadur K. V. Rangaswami Iyengar, M. A., thus writes about it in the Journal of the Benares Hindu University: Malayalam is the vernacular of about ten millions in India. Owing to the comparative isolation of the tract, not much has been known of Kerala, its inhabitants and culture, particularly in N. India.,...It is therefore a matter of satisfaction that Mr. K. M., who is well-known for his great knowledge of the history and literature of his tract, has reprinted his very popular sketch of the history of Malayalam literature published forty years ago, as a college exercise of a gifted, precocious student, with commendatory foreword by Kerala Varma, Valiya Koil Tampuran, the great scholar and poet. A more compact and readable introduction in English to the history of Malayalam literature will be hard to get, or one written with better judgment."

OF

MALAYALAM LITERATURE

THE COUNTRY WHERE MALAYALAM IS SPOKEN

Malayālam is the language of the south-west districts of the Madras Presidency. It is the third most important language of the Presidency, the first and the second being Tamil and Telugu respectively. It is spoken in Malabar, Cochin and Travancore. It is the mother-tongue of 9,137,615 persons. Malabar, Cochin and Travancore, taken as a whole, are bounded on the north by South Canara, on the east by the far-famed Malaya range of mountains, on the south by the Indian Ocean, and on the west by the Arabian Sea.

Properly speaking, Malabar is the name of a small district of which Calicut is the capital. But the term is now and then loosely applied to that tract of land which, besides the above, includes Cochin and Travancore also. The natives love to call it Kēralam and Malayālam. These names are well suited to it, the former (Kēram=cocoanut) 'on account of the dense forest of cocoanut palms which constitute the wealth of the country', and the latter (Mala= hill and ālam=dale) from the undulating nature of its surface. Other derivations are possible and are given for these place-names. But there is no need to delay over them here.

"The low belt which borders on the sea and the backwaters is by nature flat and swampy, but has in the course of ages become rich with the works of man, and the landscape shaded and fanned by 'the feathery palm' presents a chequered scene of light and shade. As we leave the seaboard, an undulating country, diversified with grassy flats, naked hills and wooded terraces, intersected by numerous torrents and rapids dashing down from cliff to valley, and profusely dotted with simple homesteads, orchards and cultivated fields, rolls up to the foot of the western ghats, where the landscape, now become nobler and more intensified in grandeur, merges itself in wide forests of continuous shade, leaving 'a woody theatre of stateliest view' amidst 'a variegated maze of mount and glen."

Geology supports the tradition which asserts that the Kerala country was raised out of the sea ; but the ancients have dressed the tradition in the garb of Paraśurāma. It is possible that the great pioneer Paraśurāma led the first Aryan settlers into Kēralam, which, long before their advent, had evolved a culture unique in its own way.

The Aryans must have found the country divided into villages or ṭaras. Each village was self-contained and consisted of houses situated in detached gardens. These villages had their own organisation for agrarian, social, civil and administrative purposes. They were in fact miniature republics so far as their civil life was concerned. It was the Ṅāṭṭār (people of the country) who administered the country with the help of the Kūṭṭam, the National Assembly. For political purposes, the country was divided into Ḍēśams and Ṅāḍḍūs under Ḍēśavālies and Ṅāḍūvālies, while, for military training, it came to be divided into 18 samghams. Each of these had six systems of training. The Kalaries or the fencing-schools were held in the vicinity of a Kāvu. That is how we find reference in hymns and old records to 108 kalaries and the same number of Ḍurgālayās in Kērala.

At one period in the political evolution of the country, the groups of villages called Ṅāḍs were placed under chieftains known as Ṭaliyāṭiries nominated for three years by special electors. There were eighteen and a half Ṭalies in Kērala, a *tali* being the area covered by the jurisdiction of a chieftain. The dissensions among the Ṭaliyāṭiries and the unrest among the people due to the bad rule of these led them to appeal to powerful, neighbouring rulers for help. This is how the Perumals, Viceroys chosen from the royal houses of Chēra, Chōla and Pāndya, came to rule over Kērala. Some of them did not rule out their term of 12 years, as a few died premature deaths, while others were replaced for their misrule. The dates of the Perumal period have not yet been definitely determined. Some give the kāli, bhūman bhūpōyam prāpa (A.D. 216) as the date of its commencement, while others state that the cryptogram ḍuḍurdharam (B.C. 113) is the correct year.

The capital of the Perumals was Ṭiruvanchikulum near Cranganur in the vicinity of the port of Muziris which Pliny calls *primum emporium Indiae.* The Egyptians, the Phoenicians, the Greeks and the Romans came to this port for commercial purposes. The Jews, the Muslims and the Christians claim Cranganur as their first settlement. There was a great university at Maṭilakam, near Cranganur, where the Viḍvalsabha, the assembly of the wise, directed the studies of the university and enacted laws for the country. It was presided over by Ilankoadigal, the author of *Silappadhikaram*, and the son of Bāṇa Varman Nētumchēralāṭan who is said to have ruled Kērala from A.C. 115 to 129 A.C. It was Ilankoadigal's friend, Chit't'alay Chāṭṭanār, that wrote *Manimekhala.* These and the *Patittippattu* by other Kērala Kavis were all published from Ṭiruvanchikulam.

Bhāskara Ravi Varma was the last of the Perumals; he turned out to be so popular and his rule so wise and just that he was permitted to rule the country for 37 years. Urudhīsamāśraya (342 A.D.), Chēramāndēsamprapa (A.D. 343), Ṣhōdaśāmgam surājyam (A.D. 385) are some of the kalis associated with his name.[1] The Malayalam kingdom was, for various reasons, partitioned, so some say, by him among his friends and relatives. Malabar, Cochin and Travancore arose out of the dismemberment of that ancient Malayalam kingdom.

From very early times, some of the products peculiar to the Malabar Coast were known to several of the nations of Asia and Europe, and were the objects of maritime enterprise and commerce throughout the succeeding centuries. "The Phoenicians by way of the Persian Gulf and, subsequently, by way of the Red Sea; the Jews under David and Solomon; the Greeks under Alexander the Great; the Syrians under the Seleucidae; the Egyptians under the Ptolemies; the Romans under the Emperors; the Arabians after the conquest of Egypt and Persia; the Italians; the Portuguese; the Dutch; the French"—each nation had its share in the trade with the Kèrala country. And it is no secret that, for the last two centuries, the English have been carrying on a brisk trade with the ancient 'land of pepper.'

[1] My friend Ullur thinks he ruled in the 10th—11th centuries of the Christian era.

From its commercial prosperity, it should not be supposed that the Malayalam territory had all along enjoyed peace. For, there are reliable records to show that, for some centuries before it came under the English sway, the country was the scene of battles, internal feuds and foreign invasions, a fact which clearly explains the slow progress of the Malayalam literature in those days and its rapid growth within the last hundred years.

Between the years 1792 and 1795 A.D., Malabar, Cochin and Travancore came under the supremacy of the British. With this supremacy came schools and books and all the paraphernalia of modern civilization, and people began to take an interest in the language, arts and industries of their ancestors. The Malayālīs took to the new system of instruction with great avidity. The result has been very remarkable. In the words of one of the Imperial Census Reports, " In education, the rate of improvement is highest in Malabar. Both Cochin and Travancore have a larger degree of education than the Madras Presidency as a whole, larger too than the adjoining district of Malabar, though this is true only of male education, so far as Travancore is concerned. The people of Cochin, both males and females, are more educated than the inhabitants of any other district except Madras." It is therefore not very strange that the Malayālīs are now taking a lively interest in the development of their language and literature.

MALAYALAM LANGUAGE

Malayālam is one of the Dravidian languages. Dravidian is from Ḍraviḍa, the adjectival form of Ḍrāviḍa. This term is a 'generic appellation of the south India peoples and their languages.'

The Dravidian cultivated languages are—

1. Tamil
2. Telugu
3. Malayālam
4. Cānarēse.
5. Tulu.
6. Koḍagu.

From the scanty materials that we possess, it is not easy to trace exactly the origin of the Malayalam language. The opinion of some great philologists seems to be that there must originally have been some dialect spoken by the tribes of Malabar. According to Mr. P. T. Sreenivasa Iyengar, the languages spoken in India in olden days were all dialects of proto-

Tamil, while Dr. Maclean, though he does not go so far, still holds that there is little doubt that the Dravidian languages are comparatively older in point of time than Sanskrit. Dr. Gundert says that Tamil and Malayalam differed as dialects of the same member of the Dravidian family. The late Chattambi Swāmi, whose encyclopaedic knowledge was the wonder and despair of his erudite contemporaries, held that Sanskrit, Samskṛṭam, is refined Tamil, or, to be more accurate, proto-Tamil. In *Lilatilakam,* a very old work on Malayalam grammar, it is shown that Maṇipravāḷam is a combination of Malayalam and Sanskrit.

The work then says that Tamil there means Malayalam. Tamil was a generic term for all Ḍrāviḍa languages in remote times. Mr. Āt't'ūr K. Pishāroti in his *Critical Survey of the Malayalam Language and Literature* shows how the term Tamil became Damiḷa, Damida, Dramida and finally Ḍraviḍa. The late A. R. Rajaraja Varma, the author of *Kerala-Paniniyam*, says in that classical work that the literary Tamil was called Chentamil, while the popular, spoken Tamil was called Kotumtamil. There were different varieties of this, one of which, Karintamil, grew to become Malayālam. Very few means are there to trace the growth of this dialect to its modern form. Separated from the old stock and its other branches by the ghauts, this variety underwent gradual changes. Sanskrit has affected the grammar and vocabulary to a great extent. It was very much influenced by Tamil, and, to a less extent, by Tulu, Canarese and Telugu. " The resultant of these forces acting upon the original dialect of Malabar is the present Malayalam Language. Terms connected with the Muhamedan religion, government and commerce have found their way into Malayalam from Arabic, Persian and Hindustani ; while Hebrew, Syriac, Greek and Latin have contributed terms connected with Christianity. A few words current in the language are derived from Portuguese, Dutch and French. English tends to influence its idioms, gives birth to new terms of expression and thus moulds the public thought into different forms."

" In the Dravidian languages all names denoting inanimate substances and irrational beings are of the neuter gender. The distinction of male and female appears only in the pronouns of the third person, in adjectives formed by suffixing the pronominal terminations, and in the third person of the verb. In all other cases the distinction of gender is marked by separate words signifying male and female. Dravidian nouns are inflected by means of suffixed post-positions and separable particles. Dravidian neuter nouns are rarely pluralised. Dravidian adjectives are incapable of declension. A peculiarity of the Dravidian dialects is the existence of two pronouns of the first person plural, one inclusive and other exclusive of the person addressed. The Dravidian languages have no passive voice. The Dravidian verbal system possesses a negative as well as affirmative voice. It is a marked peculiarity of the Dravidian languages that they make use of relative participial nouns instead of phrases introduced by relative pronouns." The chief difference between Malayalam and the other Dravidian tongues is that in the former, the verb has gradually got itself divested of all distinctions as to gender, number and person.

DIFFERENT EPOCHS

A well-known writer on Malayalam Literature divides the growth of Malayalam into four epochs :—

I. KARINTAMIL
3100 B. C.—100 B. C.

From the songs, religious and other, composed by Kulaśēkhara Ālvar, Pākkanār and others, we get an insight into the language of this period. There is a strong admixture of Tamil in it. Sanskrit had not then begun to influence it.

II. OLD MALAYALAM
100 B. C.—325 A. D.

We find innumerable Sanskrit words in the language by the close of the period. There were personal terminations for verbs, and these were conjugated for gender and number. But it is very doubtful whether this was true in the case of the spoken language. From the copper-plate deeds of this period and from the records of daily events that used to be kept in certain ruling families at this period, we see what progress the language had made by this time. It is only from this time onwards that we see compositions in prose.

III. MIDDLE MALAYALAM
325 A. D.—1425 A D

The traces of the adjuncts of verbs had disappeared by this time. The Jàins seem to have encouraged the study of the language. From the court chronicles referred to above, from *Ramacharitam* and from Kaṇṇaśśa Paṇiker's *Ramayanam*, we get a clear idea of the language of the period.

IV. MODERN MALAYALAM
1425 A. D.

By this time, Malayalam got itself entirely divorced from Tamil, and we find modern Malayalam in all its distinctness. This period may profitably be divided into two parts, the first ending about 1795 A. D., the year in which the English got complete possession of the Kerala country, the other commencing from that year.

The coolness with which these four main periods are marked off with their corresponding dates is really astonishing.

The styles of writing that were in vogue and of which we have any knowledge were the Kōleḷuṭṭu and the Vaṭṭeḷuṭṭu scripts. The present is called Malayalam *grantha* characters.

Kērala Pāṇini has suggested another division :

Early Malayalam 1 to 500 M. E. (825 A. D. —1325 A. D.)

Middle Malayalam 500 to 800

Modern Malayalam 800 and onwards.

A recent historian of Malayalam Poetical Literature has adopted this division and has clubbed together certain outstanding works under these heads.

Early Malayalam—*Ramacharitam*; *Unninili Sandesam*.

Middle Malayalam—*Champus; Chandrotsavam*: *Ramakatha; Niranam works*; *Krishnagatha*.

Modern Malayalam—Works of Ṭuñchan, Kuñchan and Pūnṭānam; those of Kōttayam Kērala Varma; of Pūmṭōṭṭam, and Chēlapparambu; those of Rāmapurath Vārier and Uṇṇāyi Vārier; *Krishnattam*: *Kathakalies* of Koṭṭārakara and Kōṭṭayam Ṭampurāns, and those of Irayi Vaṟman Ṭampi.

To these he also adds another division which he calls New Malayalam, under which he puts the works of modern poets headed by Valiya Kōil Ṭampurān and Koṭungallūr Ṭampurāns. To most of these I shall have to refer in their appropriate places in this brief sketch.

MALAYALIS WHO HAVE WRITTEN WORKS IN SANSKRIT

No sketch of Malayalam Literature can be complete which does not make mention of Malayalīs who have won renown by their works in Sanskrit. I shall therefore take a rapid survey of them. I can find space only for a few among a host of very important names. Kērala claims among her sons, Vararuchi, the great progenitor of astronomical science in Malayalam, and

Bhartṛhari, the renowned author of the three Ṣaṭakams. The early literary history of the Malayalam language contains so many stories about their doings in the land that it would be impossible for any one to believe that they were not Malayalīs. The great theologian and philosopher, Śankarāchārya, was born at Kālaṭi, on the banks of the Chūrṇi, up the Alwaye river, which in his time belonged to Cochin. His commentaries on the Upanishads, the Vēḍānṭa Sūtrās, and the Bhagavaṭ Gīṭa are well-known to the world. No Indian need be told that his system of Aḍvaiṭa Philosophy is one of the grandest products of the human genius. The great vēḍānta and mīmāmsa scholar Prabhākara too was a Malayali. He belonged to the Vēṅṅanāt grāmom, reputed for its scholars and praised for that in *Suka Sandesam.* The Prabhākara-darśanam got a firm foothold in Kerala through the sponsorship of Payyūr Bhaṭṭaṭiries. He had as one of his disciples a person from Veḷḷāngallūr in the Mukundapuram Tālūk of Cochin, who speaks of his master, in his *Manameyodayam*, a mīmāmsa work, as a master in both the mīmāmsās. He is also the author of *Govindacharitam Kavyam*, and of the commentaries to *Raghuvamsam* called Padārthadīpika, to *Kumarasambhavam* called Vivaraṇam and to *Uttararama charitam* called Bhāvārṭṭaḍīpika.

Kulaśēkhara Ālwār, the author of *Mukundamala* [1] and of the dramas of *Tapatisamvaranam*[2] and *Danamjayam* was a patron of letters. Thōlan has written *Mahodayapuracharitam*, a mahākāvya in praise of the Kulaśēkhara royal house. He is also the author of a Malayalam work on dramaturgy called *Attaprakaram* and of several humorous verses to be used at Kūtiyāttam and Samkhakkaḷi. The diction of *Attaprakaram* is imitated in *Unninili Sandesam* and by Champu writers. Kathakali also helped to popularise it.

The drama *Ascharya-Chudamani* by Śakṭibhaḍra, a disciple of Śrī Śankara, has received the blessing of that sage, while the *Krishnavijayam Kavyam* of Śankarakavi has been the object of unmeasured praise of Uḍḍaṇḍa Ṣāṣṭri. Raman Nambiyār of Vettaṭṭunād was a great

(1) and (2) Some think that these two works were written by two different authors.

favourite of Mārṭṭānda Varma of Vēṇād and of Dēvanārayaṇan of Ambalappuḷa. He wrote two mahākāvyās. His *Rasakrida and Vrutta-varttikam* are highly spoken of by scholars. *Krishnavilasam* by Sukumāra kavi and *Balabharatam* by Agasṭya kavi bid fair to compete with Kalidasa's *Kumarasambhavam* and *Raghuvamsam* respectively. *Yudhish-tiravijayam* (ayamaka kavya), a *Kavya* of a peculiar structure, is the work of Vāsudēva Bhattaṭiri. He was the son of Ravi Nampūṭiri, a friend of Kulaśēkhara Ālwār and the annotator of the two dramas of that king. Vāsuḍēva was, like Śankarāchārya, a Nampūṭiri which means a Malayāḷi Vedic Brahman. The *Kavyamala* editors have done an injustice to Malabar by ascribing the authorship of this poem to a native of Kashmere. *Vasudevavijayam* by Vasudeva Bhattaṭiri is a *Prakriyakavya* in imitation of the *Battikavya*, as a continuation of which Mēppaṭṭūr Narayana Bhattaṭiri wrote his *Dhatu-kavya*. Karinganpiḷḷi Namputiri is the author of *Suka-sandesam*. It is after the model of *Megha-sandesam*. He gives us vivid sketches of many parts of Malabar which are dear to every Malayali. Meppathur Narayana Bhattatiri a poet, grammarian and scholar of unquestioned ability is the author of *Narayaneeyam*, which treats of the life and teachings of Śrī Krishṇa as narrated in *Bhagavatham Dasamam*. It was finished in 1558. From its pathos, and the sublimity of its religious sentiment, from its pure diction and fine melody and the display of Sanskrit scholarship, it is placed in the front rank among the classics of Sanskrit literature. Sense and sound seem to be wedded in this poem of undying fame. His grammatical works, *Prakriya Sarvaswam*, is much more lucid than Battōji Dīkshiṭar's *Sidhanta Kaumudi*.

His illom was near the Chandanakāvu in Vettaṭṭunād. His father, Māṭṛḍaṭṭan Bhattaṭiri was a Vedic scholar and was learned in both the mimamsas. His mother was a sister of the seven Payyūr Bhattatiris, about the eldest of whom it was that Uḍḍanḍa Śāsṭri praised in glowing terms.

Mēppattūr Narayana Bhattaṭiri was thus related to the Payyūr Bhattatiris whose wide, varied and profound scholarship and generous hospitality are referred by Sastri in his *Kokila-*

sandesam. Sastri's *Mallika-marutam* contains an appreciation from Paramēśwaran Bhattatiri, one of the brothers who has written an annotation to *Jaimini-Mimamsa*; while another is the author of *Bhrunga-sandesam*, where Ṭṛkkandiyūr Achyuṭa Pisharoti, the author of *Pravesika* and *Bhugoladipika*, is extolled. Narayana Bhattatiri learned grammar under this Achyuta Pisharoti. Ṭalakkulaṭṭ Bhattatiri is the author of *Dasadhyayi* and *Muhurṭapadvi*.

Narayana Bhattatiri married from Trkkandiyur Pisharoti's house. Bhattatiri was a friend of Vīrakērala Varma of Cochin as evidenced by his *Matamaharajyaprasasthi*, and of Chempakaśśēri Dēvanārayaṇa at whose instance he wrote *Dhatu Kavya* and *Prakriyasarvaswam.* At the court of the latter he had as his cosadasya Mūkōla Nīlakaṇṭan Nampūṭiri, the author of *Narayaneeyam* and *Chellur-Nathodyam* champus. *Niranunasikaprabandham* was written at the request of Iravi Chākyār. *Prakriyasarvasvam* is, so to say, a miraculous work; for it was composed in two months. The difficulty and importance of the work may be gathered from the fact that no less a scholar than the late Valiya Koil Thampuran thought it worth his while to write a second commentary for it, although another one by Trkkandiyūr Govinda Pisharoti, a disciple of Ramapāṇivāḍār and Manōrama Thampurātti, already existed.

To go back to the ancients once again, there is Vilvamangalath Swāmiyār, the famous author of *Krishnakarnamrutham.* He has written a kāvyam of singular interest. It is in prākṛtam, and every slōkam serves as an example of a separate rule on the grammar of that dialect. From this any one conversant with that dialect will have an idea of the brain power of that great ascetic. He has also to his credit a commentary to *Kenopanishad,* and one to the grammatical work *Ḍaiva*, called *Purushakaram. Dipaprabha* rivals *Purushakaram.* That is the work of one Narayana, a native of Vēṅṅaṅātu. Of the learning and scholarship found in this grāmam near Ernakulam, *Sukasandesam* praises in no stinted terms. He has also written commentaries to Patañjali's *Mahabhashya* and to *Kaiyatan's Pradipam.* A member of Kāśi Illom in Ramanallūr in north

Travancore, a great grammarian himself, has written two commentaries in verse to Pāṇini's Sūṭras. *Amodam* is also a poetical commentary to Bana's *Kadambari* by one Ashtamūrṭṭi, evidently a Nampūṭiri who lived near to and to the east of Ṭṛkkaṇāmaṭilakam. When Daṇḍi, grandson of Bhāravi, was living at Kānchīpuram as the chief court poet of the Pallava ruler Simha Vishnu, he was invited by Laliṭālayan, a master of Silpasastra, to visit Mahābalipuram where, the architect seems to have told Dandi, the latter could meet great souls like Māṭṛḍaṭṭa and others from Kerala whose company would be a source of honour and of pleasure to the poet.

Mention must be made of the names of Kākkaśśeri Battathiri, the author of *Vasumati-mitram*, Manavikrama the Strong, and Rama Varmah the Learned of Kodungallur, and a host of others, great intellectual giants, who were at once the delight and despair of many an erudite scholar from other parts of India. One is tempted to linger over the names of Mānavēḍan Raja who composed the *Manaveda Champu* which treats of the stories of Mahabharata not treated in *Bharata Champu* by Ananṭakavi, of Maḷamangalam Nampūṭiri, the author of the famous Bhāṇam called after his name, and of Pāṇivāḍan, the author of the *Raghaviya kavya* and of *Sitaraghavanatakam*, and of *Vitanidra* a Bhāṇam with Mahōḍayapuram as its scene of action. They were masters of the Sanskrit tongue and owed their predominance to the towering intellectual powers which they possessed. Arūr Bhattaṭiri produced *Uttara Naishadham*, a fitting complement to the work of Sri Harsha. H. H. Rama Varma, a Maharaja of Travancore, wrote an excellent didactic poem called *Bhakthi Manjari* and also innumerable musical compositions known as Kīrṭṭanams. K. Rama Varier may be appropriately styled the Mallinātha of modern times. On various difficult works he has written commentaries. There is no subject that is foreign to him, and every subject he has treated about, he has treated in a masterly fashion. *Visakha Vijayam*, *Kamsavadha Champu*, *Pranama Satakam* and *Tulabhara Satakam* of H. H. Kerala Varma, the late Valiya Koil Thampuran of Travancore, show how elastic Sanskrit language becomes when wielded by a master-hand. They are remarkable for the felicity of their diction, the richness of their varied imagery, the skill and art displayed in the several figures of speech and for the vast sweep of his powers as a poet. From *Angala Samragyam*, one can confidently assert that his nephew and pupil, A. R. Raja Raja Varma, comes as a good second to his uncle. Kochunṇi Thampurān of Kodungallur has easily won the name of a first-class Sanskrit poet. His *Vipra Sandesam* and his *Bhanam* have cheered not a few of the erudite scholars and critics of several parts of India. Punnassēri Nambi Ṅīlacanta Śarma edited a Sanskrit Journal which reflected great credit on his Sanskrit scholarship and philanthropy, and the Sanskrit College he has started at Pattāmbi will be for ever a monument to his wide and varied erudition more enduring than any storied urn or animated bust. Another who has won renown is Pūrṇaṣarasvaṭi whose annotations of *Megha-sandesam* and *Malatì-madhavam* are considered works of unusual merit.

Towards the growth of Jyōṭisha, Kerala has contributed not a little. There used to be a

Paṇḍiṭasaḍas during the time of the Māmāmkam, which was held once in twelve years on the banks of the Bharaṭappuḷa near the Ṭirunāvāya temple, to renew kanam deeds, and to select a ruler. Among the subjects that were taken up for consideration by the assembly of the pandits, one would be the science of Jyōṭisha, with a view to make corrections and deviations to suit local conditions.

The *Balasankaram* of Maḷamangalom and the *Tantrasamgrakam* and *Aryabhatiya-bashyam* of Nīlacaṇta Sōmayāji are worthy of mention. It is of this Nilacantan that Ṭuñchath Eḷuthaššan speaks as his guru in his works. He was a native of Ṭṛikantiyūr and a dependant of the Aḷuvāncheri Mana.

In other departments too of Sanskrit learning, Malabar has never been behind other parts of India. In Ṣilpisāsṭra, it followed the mayamaṭam. Uliyannūr Perumṭachchan is a host in himself. *Tantrasamuchchayam* of Chēnnas Namputiri is a classic connected with matters relating to temples. *Vivaranam* and *Vimarsini* are two of its well-known commentaries. Kerala has made solid contributions to the science and practice of Ṭachchu Ṣāstra, Ancient temples and particularly certain Kūṭṭampalams (theatres) exist as finished products of indigenous sculpture and architecture.

The system of Āyurvēḍa as practised in Malabar bears the impress of the country. Its growth there stands unrivalled. In *Dhara* and *Pilichil* and massage, in bone-setting and the treatment of cuts and dislocations, the Kerala system is seldom excelled. It has also specialised in the treatment of elephants and poison cases. In specialisation, one finds intensive earnestness in Astronomy and Astrology and Āyurvēḍa. In what other country have you heard of Ashtavaidyans, members of eight famous, hereditary families of physicians who are ever ready to attend on the needy sick and give them their skilled services not for fame nor for money but out of the love for humanity?

A commentary in Malayalam for Kautilya's *Arthasastra*, *Arthasastrabhashyavakya*, is about 1000 years old. The late Gaṇapaṭi Ṣāsṭri based his Sanskrit commentary on this work. *Uttejini* a commentary to *Kavyaprakasam*, *Manidarpanam*, *Balaramabharatam*, and

Kanadasidhanta Chandrika are all works by Malayalis.

Before bringing this subject to a close, it will not be out of place to refer to the high standard of proficiency in Sanskrit attained by many of the members of the ruling, and several of the other aristocratic families in Malabar. This used to be so from very ancient days.

Those palaces and families were centres of Sanskrit learning. There students were fed and taught kāvyam, alamkāram and Ṣāsṭram free. Ṭṛikkaṇāmaṭilakam, Kāṇṭalūr Ṣāla, Ṣrīmūlavāsam and Ṭṛchcharanāṭṭmala, and several mutts were famous for the provision they had for the higher studies on those subjects. Until very recently, Kodungallur Rajas' family contained experts who could and did teach different subjects to aspirants for proficiency in learning. The Sanskrit Colleges at Trivandrum and Ṭṛppūṇiṭṭura, at Pattāmbi and Annakara show that the love for higher studies in Sanskrit is still strong in Kerala. Several rulers of Travancore and of Cochin were scholars and patrons of learning. A few of them wrote works of great merit. The interest the Rulers of these States take in the

Sanskrit colleges, and in the work of the Malayalam Improvement Committee in Cochin and of the Committeés to publish Sanskrit and Malayalam works in Travancore evince their interest in the maintenance of ancient culture and the development of Sanskrit and Malayalam literatures.

MALAYALAM LITERATURE

EARLY MALAYALAM TO 500 M. E.

The innumeral folk songs that have come down to us make it clear that the Malayali nation began to lisp in numbers at this early period. From these and from certain religious songs, such as *Sastham Pattu*, *Bhadra Kali Pattu*, which to this day pious souls chant to propitiate their favourite gods and goddesses, one can get an idea of the language of this period. The one note-worthy work of this time is *Ramacharitam*, said to be the work of a Raja of Travancore. He composed it, it is said, as a *patappattu*, a martial song, to be sung by soldiers when they went out for battle. There is only thus the *Yuddha khandam* in it. What original he followed for his rendering, it is difficult to surmise. The admixture of Tamil in the language used in it is so pronounced that certain Tamil scholars class it as a Tamil work. This it is not. That Tamil lent its colour to the language of that period is seen from *Unninilisandesam*, an admittedly Malayalam classic. That is a remarkable poem. Materials for history, geography and social life of that period can be gleaned from it. Its texture, its ideas and imagery are themes for admiration among modern poets and scholars, while among these the authorship and the identity of the messenger are still contentious matters.

It is a matter for congratulation to the Malayalīs that prose literature also was cultivated in this period; for prose is an essential factor in the progress of civilization. The copper-plate grants of Vīrarāghava Chakravarṭi show where Malayalam prose stood in those days.

MIDDLE MALAYALAM
500—800 M. E.

Many songs were composed during this period for the people to sing when they sowed and reaped and when they engaged themselves in work and worship. Some of them are popular even in these days. Here in Kerala too as elsewhere the people had their feasts of music and dance: the songs that welcome the birth of a child, those to rock the cradle; the bridal songs; 'the ballads to chronicle the deeds of their heroes; their chorus-songs for their golden harvests; their solos for the lovers to sing; the mystic hymns of the rustic saints.' These show the heart-beats of the village life and culture. Some of these songs are very popular even now as *Kaikottikkalippattus*; so also are certain ballads called *Vadakkanpattus*. Of these the most popular are *Thachchȯlippattus*. These narrate the gallant exploits of Mēppayil Kuñhi Oṭēnan, a valiant Nayar of Ṭachchōli, a village in the Kurumbranad Taluk in North Malabar. These display the life of the Malayalīs of those days in a realistic manner, of their rough and ready ways, and of their bold and straight dealings, and also clearly indicate the stage in the development of the language. One notes a great advance in these from the days of *Ramacharitam*, and *Ramakatha* and *Mavaratam pattus*.

Pāttu means a song in Dravidian metre. It has several varieties: *Krishippattu, Kalameluttupattu, Velanpattu, Pananpattu, Tantunippattu, Bhadrakalìppattu, Brahmanippattu, Sastrakkalippattu Sasthampattu, Purappattu, Onappattu, Tiruvatirappattu, Vanchippattu,* and number of other varieties.

Many pāttus (songs) are devotional or had their origin in connection with ceremonies performed in temples. The Kerala Temples always stood not only for the cultivation of the spiritual life but also and more 'for the administration of charity, the dissemination of education, the encouragement of fine arts and the employment of a great number of people.' Some of them show "the wonderful development that the country has reached in architecture, sculpture and iconology. The paintings on the walls and panelled ceilings are marvels of art. Temples are also centres of festive gatherings. During the time of these festivals, there will be processions, dancing and drumming, music and piping, drama, *Kuttu* and *Fatakam* and sports of various sorts........The songs that accompany the sports and dances, the dramatic literature and the hymnology which are the outcome of these temples are of a high order. Many of these are rightly ranked as classics." The perfection of the drumming, dancing and the music of Kerala have reached a stage which is beyond the pale of controversy.

The poems of Niraṇaṭṭu Paṇikkars are compositions of no mean merit. Their *Ramayanam*, *Bharatam* and *Bhagavatgita* appeal to the ear and to the mind.

The history of the Malayalam language, observes a writer, 'commences, if inscriptions on copper and stone are omitted, with the *Ramacharitam*, the oldest Malayalam poem extant. Composed as it was before the Sanskrit alphabet (*Malayala grantha* characters) came into existence it is deserving of notice, as it exhibits the earliest phase of the alphabet, probably very many centuries before the Portuguese.'

Cheruśśēri Nampūṭiri, the morning star of Malayalam ṣong, lived in this epoch. It was a fortunate day for Keralam when one of the Namputiries, a class of people who then professed to dislike the Malayalam tongue, began to compose in that language. But this is the least important recommendation for *Krishnagatha* for our acceptance. For, the work, considered even on other grounds, has scarcely been surpassed by similar writings of subsequent days. It has raised the status of the Malayalam language. The poet had a keen eye for beauty and knew how to express it in words that catch the fancy and touch the heart of man. It is a monumental piece of work and has rightly raised its author to that 'kingly breed who starry diadems attain.'

It was Cherusseri who first showed that, if he is so minded, a great poet can practise his art in Malayalam without a large admixture of Sanskrit words. He was followed by Punam, Pūmṭānam and Chēlapparambu, and latterly by the Venmaṇis and the two great Cranganore poets.

It should have been stated before this that almost all the poetical pieces of Malayalam are written in what is called Maṇipravālam which means a string of gems and corals. It receives its name from being composed in a mixture of Malayalam and Sanskrit words. The addition, here and there, of common Sanskrit words only gives grace and majesty to Malayalam which otherwise would be bald. It is, therefore, to be understood that there is nothing of the Babylonish dialect about *manipravalam.* The metres of the Malayalam ślōkams are the same as those of the Sanskrit ones; and those that are peculiar to the language, as in the case of the famous works of Ṭunjan and Kunjan, are known and distinguished by their *matras*, the time required to utter them.

Cherusseri wrote his *gatha* in simple, graceful Malayalam so as to be appreciated not by the learned alone but to be easily understood by the masses as well. It is significant that, about the same time, a class of works, called Champus, came into existence which could be understood and appreciated by the learned only. *Gadyapadyamayam Kavyam* is *champu*—that is the definition; but even the *gadya* (prose) has an affinity to *padya* (poetry). The language employed is maṇipravālam; the poets love to speak of it as '*madhura-madhura-bhasha-smaskrtanyonya - sammelana - surabhila - kavya*; but in certain places it will be pure

Sanskrit, while in rare instances, it will be pure Malayalam. Prākṛṭ of both one can meet with in these works. The authors freely use ideas and language of old poets. After the *Bhoja* (*Ramayana*) *Champu* and Ānaṇḍa Bhatta's *Bharata Champu*, Malayalis have written Sanskrit Champus, like ***Rajasuyam***, *Kiratam* and *Niranunasikam* of Meppattur Bhattathiri. The first two, *Ramayana Champu* and *Bharata Champu*, have been rendered into Malayalam by Kataṭṭanāt Krishna Vāriar and Chunakkara Uṇṇi Krishna Variar respectively. The latter has also done into Malayalam the *Nirnunasikam*. But the number of ***manipravala Champus*** is legion. *Ramayana Champu*, *Bharata Champu*, *Chellurnathodayam* of Punam Namputiri, and ***the*** *Bhashanaishada Champu* and *Rajaratnavaliyam* of Maïamangalam (Mahishamangalam) are worthy to be mentioned here. The authors of these were gifted poets and had an amazing power of expression. Among the moderns who have successfully attempted this sort of composition are the late Ravi Varma, the author of *Ushakalyanam*, Rao Sahib Ullur Parameswara Iyer, M.A., B.L., who wrote *Sujatodvaham* and Mr. P. Sankaran Nambiyar, M.A., who is responsible for *Palazhimadhanam.* From the language and the contents one would regard these as the works of ancient and not of modern poets. Mr. Sankaran Nambiyar is also the author of a fine history of Malayalam Literature, and also of a few poetical works which are sufficient to indicate his scholarship and poetical skill.

Chandrotsavam is a remarkable product of the *Champu* period. It is not a *champu*, but its language is very like that used in *champus*. As a work of art it stands in the front line. It narrates the incidents of a village festival. Some take it as a work that depicts the rural life of the day in a northern district of the State of Cochin. There may be some substance in the contention. But the statement does not represent the whole truth. For it will be clear from the poem that the gifted poet has drawn largely on his imagination for the development of the appropriate *rasas*.

Certain Naṃbutiṭiries who had, in ancient times, suffered social degradation, formed themselves into a separate caste called Chākkiyars. Their duty was to tell Pauranic stories in an impressive way to the people who assembled to hear them. " They recite sacred legends before large audiences ; they amuse and entertain their hearers by their wit, or move them to laughter or to tears by their eloquence; and they thus teach the public in the traditions of the past, and preserve from age to age the literary heritage of the nation." In doing so, they are permitted to make the defects and bad traits of the community the butt of their sarcasm and satire which oftentimes operate as a healthy corrective. Their women, Nangyars, sit by their side and beat two metal gongs, while the Nambiyar help them in the play by beating a big drum.

MODERN MALAYALAM

800 M. E.—

The one name that shines forth with exceptional splendour in the literary firmament of Keralam is that of Tunchathu Rāmānujan Eluthachchan, a man of the Nayar caste. " The Nambutiri Brahmans envied his genius and learning and are said to have seduced him by the arts of sorcery into the habit of inebriety, wishing to overshadow the mental powers which they feared. The poet, however triumphed over the habit, though he could not abandon it, and, in revenge against those whom he considered to be the cause of his debasement, opposed himself openly to the prejudices and intolerance of the Brahmans. The mode of vengeance which he chose was the exaltation of the Malayalam tongue, declaring it as his intention to raise it to an equality with the sacred language of the God and the Rishis. In the prosecution of this purpose he enriched the Malayalam language with the translations of *Ramayanam*, *Mahabharatam* and *Bhagavatam*" These are called Kili-pāttus (parrot-songs) of Eluthachchan, who was the first to introduce this sort of composition into the Malayalam language. They receive this name from the introductory invocation to the bird of the Goddess of Learning which these works contain. Other causes also one can easily be given for the name. Of him and his works, we can only speak with reverential admiration. His works are even now considered models for imitation. Not a page is there in his works which does not contain passages glowing with religious eloquence or gleaming with wordly wisdom which lend itself at once to citation and repetition. He was an intensely religious man, and his prayers to and praises of the supreme God in which his work abound have never failed to raise the sympathetic thrill of religious enthusiasm in the mind of him who reads or sings them. He has spent the rare gifts of a genius in his strenuous service to elevate his language, to proclaim to us in new words, 'the mighty hopes that make us men'; and, therefore, it is not too much to say that his name shall be 'an echo and a light unto eternity.'

He has written many works besides the three already referred to. He also adopted Aryan script in the place of Vatteḷuṭṭu. He had many disciples who too have composed numerous works, some of which are of lasting merit. His first and last disciples were Karuṇākaran Eḷuṭṭaśśan, the author of *Bramhandapuram* and Sūryanārāyaṇan Eḷuṭṭaśśan, the author of *Parvatisvayamvaram*. In this connexion reference must be made to the name of

Eḷuvaṭṭu Nāṇukutti Menon of Chittur (b. 1835 A. D.) who, by his translation of *Ekadesam*, has shown how much he has caught of the literary spirit and religious fervour of his great forerunner Eluthachchan. *Nachiketacharitam* of Kōttūr Unniṭṭan requires a reference here. Unṇāyi Vārier's *Girijakalyanam* too is a good kiḷippāṭṭu, so too the *Vetalacharitam* of Raghava Pisharoti. Kerala Varma Raja of North Kottayam is the author of *Ramayanam* and *Vairagyachandrodayam*. *Ramayanam* is a free rendering of the immortal work of Valmiki.

Kathakali or the Malayalam Drama is one of the most intensely national departments of our literature. This branch may be the result of the natural development of *Purakkalli*, *Mohiniyattam*, *Ashtapadiyattam* and *Kutiyattam*. The episodes of *Ramayanam* and *Mahabharatam* form the subjects for these dramas. The verses simply connect the incidents of the story, while the *padams* represent the dialogues of the characters of the play. The actors, representing the several personages, generally paint their faces and dress in a peculiar fashion.

They, by means of appropriate (*mudras*) gestures, convey to the audience the meaning of the prose portions when they are sung to the accompaniment of the beating of drums and other instruments. No doubt some of these pieces, when sung by clever singers without the accompaniment of the discordant sounds of drums and metal gongs, bring with them such charm and inexpressible delight to the hearer as may 'dissolve one into ecstasies or bring all Heaven before one's eyes.'

In the *Kathakali* and the *Kutiyattam*, acting has reached its acme of perfection. It is time that the Kathakali is made more popular and understandable by the masses than now, and acceptable even to those carping but cultured critics who consider the performance 'a compound of noise and nuisance only tolerable if not too loud.'

There is so much misconception about this art of Kathakali that it will be worth the trouble to extract here what an English lady and a well-known Indian Weekly have to say on this subject. Miss Alice Bonner writes: "In Kathakali, legend and mythology come actually to life........It has preserved, alone among the arts of India, the fulness, the vitality, and the passion of life, to which ancient poetry, paintings and sculptures bear testimony........It is a dance-play, a kind of pantomime in which the actors represent the stories by means of gestures, facial expressions and dance-movements, interpreted by songs and attuned to the rhythm of drums, cymbal and gongs......There are no stage-settings to depict the situation........By the eloquence of his hand-gestures, his body movement and facial expressions, he has to convey to his audience not only the mood and the action of the play, but also the situation in which it takes place..... Kathakali has been found to be a living demonstration of all the principles laid down in *Bharat Natya Sastra*......From the composition of the drama to the dress, the steps, the 'mudras' and the smallest quiver of an eye, everything is governed by hard and fast rules."[1] *The Illustrated Weekly of India*[2] has a very informing article by one who also seems to have mastered the subject in all its

1. The *Hindustan Times*, April 1, 1936.
2. Of 28th June, 1936.

aspects. "Kathakali is the growth of ages. The primitive, classical, medieval and modern strands that adorn its rich fabric tell the evolution of Natya Sastra. The Kerala Theatre is a combination of Kuttu, Krishnanattam, Mudiyattam, Mohiniyattam and Tullal. A combination of facial expressions, hand gestures and dancing renders the language of the tongue useless. The mudras project the idea, the bhavas enliven it. Every limb and muscle of the artist has its appropriate and significant movement....This descriptive and realistic method renders the comprehension of gesture symbols easy, while the text of the drama sung by the musicians assist intelligent appreciation. No scenic settings are provided. The actors must conjure up before the audience all the scenic effects required. ....Suppose it is the story of Kuchela. Let us think of one scene. Kuchela, the poor Brahmin, a devotee and classmate of Sri Krishna, sets out at dawn to Dwaraka to meet the Lord. In the morning, he performs his ablutions. Step by step he gets into the water of the tank, splashes it with his palm; bathes, puts on holy ashes and performs his prayers. Then he ascends and starts on his journey. All this is enacted on a bare piece of ground, a few feet away from the squatting audience. Not one of them realises it all an illusion and acting till the actor leaves the stage."

The poet who invented this sort of composition was a Rajah of Kottārakara family. The subjects of his dramas are the episodes of *Ramayanam*. There is a tradition connected with the origin of *Kathakali*. The then Zamorin of Calicut, for some reason or other, refused to send his troupe of artists to the southern parts to enact *Krishnanattam*. The inventor of *Kathakali* produced his first work to make light of the decision of his northern compeer, and called it *Ramanattam* in contradistinction to *Krishnanattam*, the subject of his pieces being taken from *Ramayanam*.

But the *Kathakali* works that still captivate the minds of the educated people and capture the hearts of even the illiterate are the *Nalacharitam* of Uṇṇāyi Vārier (b. 1740), the *Uttarasvayambaram*, the *Kichakavadhom* and the *Dekshayagam* of Iravivarman Ṭampi

(b. 1783 A. D.); the *Bakavadham*, the *Kalyanasaugandhikam* and the *Krimira-vadham* of Kōttayaṭṭu Ṭampuran, the *Raja-suyam* of Kārṭika Ṭirunāl Mahārājā (1724-98 A. D.). The *Narakasuravadham* and the *Ambarishacharitam* of Aśvaṭi Ṭirunāl Mahārājā (1756-88 A. D.) and the *Ravana-vijayam* of Vidvān Kōil Tampuran (b. 1812) also still hold the stage. It is needless to name all, and profitless too. But it may be of interest to note that, while some are fit to be staged, others are fit to be sung, and yet a third set is good for both. Tampi's works eminently fit in with this third class.

Besides *Kilippattu* and *Kathakali*, there is another department of Malayalam Literature which is also entirely indigenous to Kerala; and that is the *Tullal.* Its origin is amusing. A certain Chākyār made a Nampiyār the object of much clumsy ridicule for not doing his duty properly. The latter retorted upon the Chākyār in a singular way. The next day, just when he began his performance, the Nampiyār, in an adjoining place, produced another piece which attracted such a large crowd that the Chākyār was left alone. The Nampiyār was no other than Kalakkath Kunjan Nampiyār, and the work that he performed was a *Tullal.* Indignation maketh verse it is said; and the proverb has come to be true.

Mr. V. M. Kuttikrishna Menon has given in his *Kerala Natana Kala* another version of the origin of *Tullals.* That seems to be more plausible than the one given above. Kunjan Nambiyār was a dependent of the Ambalappuḷa Raja's family, and lived there for some time. In the invocatory verses in certain of his works, Nampiyār refers to the deity of the Ṭakiliyil temple which is about two miles from Ambalappuḷa. In that temple, for 12 days from the 1st of Medam every year, there is a festival called Paṭayaṇi, at which the villagers divide themselves into parties that will compete with each other in military formations, in mock fights and in burlesque and buffoonery. Māṭṭūr Panikkar, the Prime Minister of Ambalappuḷa Raja, got Nampiyār to compose many *Tullals* for the artists and combatants to sing on that occasion. These lines, in the *Sabhapravesam Tullal* give colour to the theory:

"*bhata-ganangatay natuvilulloru*
patayanikkiha cholluwan
vativiyannoru charu-kerala-
bhasha tannay chitam varu."

"*Tullals*, literally dances, are sung to the accompaniment of music, pantomime and dancing There are three classes of *Tullals* : *Oattan, Seethankan and Parayan* ; but as the poems of the first class predominate, the poems of other classes are also termed *Oattans*. They are based mostly on the episodes of *Bharatam* and *Ramayanam*. *Oattan Tullal,* as the name indicates (*Oattan*-running), consists of a variety of rapid metres well-suited for amusing narratives. The pure *Oattan* is more vigorous than *Seethankan*, while the *Parayan* is the best suited for pathetic style. *Nalacharitam and Kiratam* are instances of the first class, *Kalyana Saugandhikam* is an example of the second set, while *Gajendramoksham* and *Sabhapravesam* form instances of the third sort of Tullals." All these *Tullals* are the works of the Nampiyār who invented this sort of composition. Besides fifty or sixty *Tullals*, he has composed nine Malayalam dramas, *Pancha-*

tantram, *Sri Krishna Charitam*, *Pathinnalu Vritham*, parrot-songs and poems in different kinds of metres.

From the wide extent of his literary activity, it should not be supposed that his works have suffered in quality. Kunjan Nampiyār is second only to Ṭunjath Eḷuṭṭachchan. Those who have not read the works of these authors and carefully collated the rules which they have laid down in their compositions are considered to be incompetent to speak with any authority on Malayalam Literature. Cochinites can legitimately feel proud that the birth-places of these in their days belonged to Cochin. About 940 M. E. Kiḷḷikuriśśi temple which Nampiyār praises in his works was renovated by the then Raja of Cochin.

Patricians aud plebians alike joined to do honour to Kunjan Nampiyār. He was under the special patronage of the Maharajah who began to adorn the throne of Travancore in the year A. D. 1758, and who, besides being a man of letters, greatly encouraged literary men of all parts of Malabar.

There is a strong individuality about his works. From any collection of quotations, his lines could be easily picked out. The cadences of the verses are perfect. His verses flow with a grace and elegance that are charming indeed ; now and then, they are spirited ; at other times they rise to an indignant and dignified eloquence; here and there, are passages of keen sarcasm. His works are strewn with jewels that will sparkle for ever.

He was the censor of the age ; he had a profound scorn for humbug and sham ; and against all such things he has directed his acid epigrams. His allusive satire on popular morals and manners must have had its biting effect on the people beyond the power of rod or sermon. He loved Malayalis and, therefore, wished to direct them in the way that they should go. Kunjan Nampiyār was nothing if not humorous. His humour, warm and all-embracing, 'bathed his ideas in a genial and abiding light.'

Two others of Nampiyār's family have contributed works to our literature. Rāghavan Nampiyār is the author of *Sakuntalam Kathakali*, and Dāmodaran Nampiyār composed *Ekadesimahatmyam*[1] and *Vilvapuranam Kilippattus.*

[1] Some are of opinion that this work is by Kunjan Nampiyar himself.

During this golden age of our national literature, there were others who worked to give a lead and to add to the output. Of many of these, only a few *slokams* remain to remind us of their having lived and to make us regret that there are not more of that sort. Pūmṭōttam and Chēlapparambu, Etapattikād and Machchātt Eḷayaṭu and Kōttūr Unṇittān belong to this class. Many assert that the *Tullal Kalakeya-vadham*, is a work of the first. Pūnṭānam and Rāmapāṇivāḍan have left much that have enriched our language. The *Bashakarnamrtam Jnanappana* and *Santanagopalam Pana* of the former are popular even to-day, and that fact speaks volumes in their favour. He was a true *bhakta*, a pure devotee whose *Karnamrtam* will not fail to touch a sympathetic chord even in those among the moderns who consider they can change their creed as their dress. While Pūntānam was a devotee of Sri Krishna, Rāmapāṇivāḍa was an adherent of Sri Rama. He has composed many hymns about that Deity. His other important works are *Raghaviyam, Vishnuvilasam* and *Sitaraghavam* in Sanskrit and *Vishnugeeta* and *Panchatantram* in

Malayalam. Though Rāmapuraṭṭu Vārier has not left much, his *Kuchelavrtam* boat-song was considered a marvel even by his contemporaries.

OUR OWN TIMES

In writing of the very modern epoch, it is not my intention to refer to the names of the several writers: they and their works are legion. In the case of living writers, I am alive to the perils of selection and exclusion, and to the difficulty of giving estimates of works yet unfinished. One discerning writer has said that to step into the field of the moderns is to step into a battlefield. I do not go so far. But, anyway, I shall be on my guard. I shall only attempt to point out a few of the manifold forces that have been at work since the advent of the English rule to improve and to develop the Malayalam language; and, while doing so, I may, now and then, say a word or two of those who have been foremost in originating or directing such forces for the good of Malabar. To attempt anything more than this would be impossible.

The year 1795 saw the establishment of the English supremacy in Malabar. With the commencement of the rule of this civilized nation, the Malayalis began to enjoy, with but few exceptions, uninterrupted peace and prosperity. It is not, therefore, strange that we see a vigorous impetus given, at this period, to the growth of the Malayalam Literature.

The Christian missionaries were the first to enter the field, and their schools and printing presses have contributed not a little to the development of the language and the literature of Keralam. The first printing press in India was established on the Malabar Coast by Christian missionaries. The dictionaries and grammars which they have made to aid those engaged in studying this language, display an amount of labour, research and erudition that is simply marvellous. And even where they have gone wrong, they have done so not because they lacked care or diligence, but because they have not been able to rightly interpret the spirit of the language. In this connection, the late Rev. Gundhert's name comes prominently to my mind. Whatever may be the defects of his *Malayalam*

Grammar, it is a veritable storehouse of information; while his dictionary of the Malayalam language is a monument of his intelligence and perseverance. It is no matter for surprise that the Malayalis venerate the name of the man who spent the best years of a long and laborious life to discover and develop the resources of their mother-tongue. Malayali scholars like Pāchu Mūṭṭaṭu and Kōvuṇṇi Nedungādi have imitated his example and have produced each a capital work on the grammar of the Malayalam language. The work of the latter is in verse and covers a large field. It is a wonderful work, his *Kerala Kaumudi*. But the best of the existing work on the subject is *Kerala Panineeyam* by the late A. R. Rajaraja Varma. He was a great Sanskrit scholar, a sound logician, and a profound glottologist and his book, 'in spite of its errors both of omission and commission, generally satisfies the criterion of a good scientific grammar.' His *Sabdusodhini*, *Sahitya-sahyam*, *Vrtta-manjari* and *Bhashabhushanam* are other works of great merit intended to develop the language and literature of Malayalam. He has also enriched the literature by his translations of *Meghdutu*, *Kumarasambhavam*, *Sakuntalam*, *Malaviganimitram* and *Charudatta*. His commentary to *Nalacharitam Kathakali* and to his uncle's rendering of *Sakuntalam* are models in that line. Messrs. T. C. Parameswaran Mūssad, Mahadeva Sarma, L. A. Ravi Varma, P. Padmanabha Menon and Srimaṭi A. Meenakshi Amma are a few among others who have enriched Malayalam literature with valuable commentaries.

I think it is proper to mention here the name of Govinda Pillai, the author of the *History of Malayalam Literature*. The amount of patience and perseverance he has shown in collecting and arranging the materials comprised in his work is marvellous, remembering that people in these parts, like the proverbial dog in the manger, refuse to give up any manuscript in their possession. Mr. P. Sankaran Nāmbiyar, Mr. R. Narayana Panikkar, and Viḍwān T. M. Chummār are others who have written works on this same subject.

The inauguration of a system of University education, such as at present obtains in this Presidency, has led to important results. In the curriculum of studies for the different examinations, the University has given a high place to the several vernaculars of the Presidency. Thus the Malayalis who are trained in English schools not only imbibe western modes of thought but are also intelligently instructed in the Malayalam language. These Malayalis, in their turn, begin to publish old and useful books, to produce new ones and to translate into Malayalam the important works of English master-minds, as also to disseminate the seeds of education throughout the length and breadth of the country. Women also have begun, as of old, to occupy their proper place in society. In every nook and corner of Keralam, one meets with schools and even colleges for girls. Many young ladies of respectable families possess every desirable accomplishment. There were many ladies in Malabar who were celebrated for their Sanskrit scholarship or for their systematic knowledge of the science of music. "Nor are feminine authors wanting in the country. The names of Manorama Tampuratti, Kutti Kunhi Tamkachchi and Ikkavu Amma are only a few out of hundreds of talented authoresses still unknown to fame."

Ikkavu Amma's *Subhadrarjunam* is the first dramatic work by a Malayali lady. Even apart from this fact, it is worthy of a high place among dramatic works. It has gone through several editions already. Ṭaravath Ammālu Amma and Śrīmathi T. B. Kalyani Amma and Srimathi T. C. Kalyani Amma are other lady writers who have enriched Malayalam literature in no small measure. What is more, their racy style has such a grace and charm about it that it has served as models for others. *Bhakta-mala*, *Budha-charitam*, are a few of the great works of Ammalu Amma. *Vyala-vattasmaranakal* of Srimathi T. B. Kalyani Amma is a very popular work. *Amma Rani*, *Visha-Vrksham* and *Krishnakanta's Will* of Srimathi T. C. Kalyani Amma are well-known in Kerala.

Princes have not been slow to recognise the altered conditions of the times. The names of Rama Varma Maharajah and his brother will be honoured by posterity as the patrons of Malayalam Literature at the time of its revival. The name of the latter has already been immortalized in *Visagha Vijayam*, a *Kavyam* in Sanskrit by His Highness the late Kerala Varma, Valia Koil Tampuran of Travancore.

This Koil Tampuran was the first to translate a Sanskrit dramatic work into Malayalam. His translation of *Sakuntalam* is not free from a few faults, and no one was readier to own them than the translator himself. It is, however, a true and dignified rendering of the original. Its popularity is unquestioned; it has reached its fourth edition, an honour paid only to one or two recent works in Malayalam. It is impossible to exaggerate the effect of this work as a guide and as a stimulant. Since 1881, the year in which *Bhasha-Sakunthalam* was published, up to the present, no less than four score dramas have seen the light of day.

During his life-time, his nephew and pupil, A. R. Rajaraja Varma published a Malayalam rendering of *Sakuntalam*. After him, recently, two other translations by Messrs. A. Krishna Pisharoti and Vallathōle Narayana Menon have been published. Will these displace the time-honoured version of Valia Kōil Tampuran? Let Time decide that question.

Another work of his, *Mayura Sandesam*,

by the beauty of its sentiments, the melody of its verse and the intensity of feeling to which it gives expression, has reached the high-water mark of Malayalam poetry. It is after the *Cloud-Messenger* of Kalidasa. But Valia Koil Tampuran has one distinct advantage over the bard of Ujjayini. In *Mega Dutha*, Kalidas only shaped what his imagination bodied forth; while the thoughts of the *Peacock-Messenger* are those that have passed through the crucible of our poet's personal experience. Even in the case of this poem, as in the case of the former work of his, critics were not wanting who think that the language of the poem is a great deal too Sanskritic. Sanskrit or not Sanskrit, 'it is poetry and magnificent poetry from the first line to the last poetry, such as there is not, perhaps, more than a small volumeful in all languages.' *Amarukasatakam*, *Anyapadesa-satakam*, *Hanumadubhavam* are some of his other poetical works in Malayalam. Besides *Visagavijayam kavyam*, he has written several other works in Sanskrit too.

As President of the Vernacular Text-book Committee of Travancore, he did yeomen service to the cause of Malayalam prose literature. His *Akbar*, one of the best prose works in Malayalam, is published under the auspices of this Committee. He was also President of the *Bhasa Poshini Sabha*, a society whose avowed object was the encouragement and development of the language and literature of Malabar.

He is to a certain extent instrumental in giving a healthy tone to prose literature, and writers are beginning to understand the imperative necessity that there is for prose compositions as well to follow certain definite rules.

His unique devotion to literature was recognised by Her Majesty's Government, by the local University and by learned Societies in England. He was a liberal patron of literature and art, and was revered by his contemporaries.

The work of translation started by Koil Tampuran was taken up by Chāṭṭukkutty Maṇṇātiyār, Kuñhi Kudtan Tampuran, Kochuṇṇi Tampurān, Vaḷḷathōle, Kundūr Narayana Menon, Kottārāṭṭil Śankuṇṇi and others. Mannātiyār was a veteran in the art of translation, and his *Uthara-Rama-Charitam* as well as his *Janaki-parinayam* and *Halasyam* display the rare abilities he possessed as a translator and poet. Kuñhikudtan Ṭampurān was a voluminous writer. No less than eight dramas, not to speak of several other works, are to be put down to his credit. There was an ease and facility about his making verses which was phenomenal. He translated the whole of *Mahabaratam* in an incredibly short time. He was called Kerala Vyāsan after that. His renderings of the *Suka-Kokila Sandesams* are beautiful, while his *Keralam* is valuable from the standpoint of history as well.

The ease he possessed in making verses has, to a slight extent, brought with it a corresponding degree of carelessness. But it must be said to his credit that he was one who was ever ready to further the cause of literature. He was a good Sanskrit scholar. His best work is his Malayalam rendering of *Ascharya Chudamani*. Though ignorant of English, he has, with the help of a friend of his, done *Hamlet* into Malayalam. Mr. Ṡankuṇṇi is, no doubt, incapable of soaring to ṭhe heights of Kuñhi Kudtan Tampuran. But he was more careful, more methodical in his work than his friend. His translation of *Vikrama* and *Urvasi* is a good piece of work, better than the rendering of the same by Kunhi Kudtan Tampuran. His translations of *Adhyatma-Ramayanam* and *Malati-Madhvam* are much appreciated by the scholars. But his most popular work is an original drama called *Kuchela Gopalam*. The periodicals of the present day are also greatly indebted to Mr. Sankunni. Some of his contributions to them have been collected in seven or eight volumes under the name of *Aithihyamala*. The easy, graceful style of prose he has adopted and the variety of interesting topics dealt with by him have made the volumes very popular among the young and the old alike.

Kochuṇṇi Ṭampurān of Kodungallūr was one of the best poets of his day. His vast and varied learning, his retentive memory, his poetic talent and his cultured tastes are even to this day topics of constant conversation among those who knew this prince. His *Kalyani* is the first original dramatic composition in Malayalam. It portrays the Malayali society of the present day and indicates the spirit of the times. He is the author of some other dramas and several works both in Sanskrit and Malayalam. His *Viprasandesam*, *Kollam* and *Bhadrolppathi* may here be referred to as examples of his works. He has also rendered *Bhagavatam* into Malayalam in the *gatha* metre. *Gosrisadityā-Charitam* and *Vanchisavamsam* are two *Mahakavyas* by him. Every Malayali will gratefully acknowledge that he was one of those few who by precept and example have improved the tone of the Malayalam poetical literature of the day. He was great in other walks of life as well.

Venmaṇi Nampūripāds, father and son, and Ravi Varma Raja belonged in their time to the band of great poets referred to above. It is impossible for any Malayali to speak of them without rapture. Some of their *slokams*, the most captivating productions of Malayalam poetry, have shown the capabilities of Malayalam. Nay more; they have fully emphasised the truth of the saying *Poeta nascitur non fit*, and have won for them, a sovereign station in the history of Malayalam Literature. The works of Venmanis have been collected and edited in three volumes by Mr. C. Achyuta Menon and myself. *Ushakalyanam*, *Champu*, *Aryasatakam*, and *Kavisabharanjanam* drama of Ravi Varma are also in print. Before I close this part of the sketch, I wish to refer to the names of K. C. Kēśava Pillai, Kaviyūr Raman Nambiyar, Sivōlli and Oravankara Nampūṭiris, and N. Rama Kurup. The works of Kesava Pillai show that he was a scholar and born poet. His drama *Raghava Madhavam* and his *Mahakavya*, *Kesaviyam*, are meritorious works, while his *Bhasha Narayaneeyam* was considered a marvel from the pen of a young poet as he then was. His *Kerala Varmah Vilasam*, a *Kavyam* on the life of the author of *Mayura Sandesam*, reflects great credit on his Sanskrit scholarship. Kaviyur Raman Nampiyar was a very bright, promising young poet. But cruel fate did not permit him to live long. He has done *Malamangala Bhanam*, *Subhadradhananjayam* and *Sri Krishna Vilasam* into Malayalam. These fruits of his, though 'gathered ere their prime' were not wanting in 'the quickness and sweetness which come of years.'

Chit't'ūr Varavūr Ṡāmu Mēnōn, a good poet, belonged to the land of Eḷuṭṭachchan. His *Yogavasishtam*, *Devi Bhagavatam* and *Tripurarahasyam*, *Atbhutharamayanam* have become popular works in Malabar. The works of

Sivolli and Oravankara Namputiris have fortunately been collected and published by their grateful and discerning relatives. Though by nature unobtrusive, their works have contributed in no small degree to direct the course of Malayalam literature. Sivolli's *Datyuha Sandesam* it was that put a stop to the production of trashy *Sandesams*. They were scholars. The works of K. C. Narayanan Nambiyar, V. C. Balakrishna Panikkar, K. Kesavan Nayar and others must be classed as fine poetry, such as of those of born poets.

When Rama Kurup wrote his *Chakee Chankaram*, there were coming into print so many dramas and poems which were drivel and unmitigated trash, not worth the paper and ink spent on them. But the satirical hits and withering sarcasm of Rama Kurup's burlesque put an end to that 'hopeless bog of poesiless verse'.

C. Anthappayi, a writer of some eminence was the author of *Sanmarga-prakasika* and *Darmopadesika*. He also directed his vitriolic ridicule against these poesiless effusions.

It will be interesting and perhaps profitable as well to take a brief but a general survey of the several departments of the Malayalam literature of recent times instead of making references to individual writers and their works. From this we shall also be able to discover in some measure the general tendencies of the age.

At one time it was thought that the art of *Kathakali* was languishing and that it might disappear from the stage. But the *Kalamandalam* started by Vaḷḷaṭṭōḷe resuscitated it in a remarkable manner, and well-known artists are coming from distant lands to learn at his Institute the technique of this wonderful art. Vallathole has put his whole heart in the scheme, and he is a name to be reckoned with. He is a great poet. He has rendered Valmiki's *Ramayanam* into Malayalam, besides several of the plays of Bhāsa. He has composed a *Mahakavyam* called *Chitrayogam.* Some of his small poetical pieces are gems that are likely to sparkle for ever on the forefinger of time. The late Ruler of Cochin whose lamented demise took place at Madras conferred on him the title of Kavisārvabhauman. He has written a *Kathakali* work. Other moderns too, like Kesava Pillai, Padmanabha Kurup, Padmanabha Panikkar and Mr. T. C. Achyuta Menon, have produced *Kathakali* compositions.

Kilippattus too have not suffered much under adverse mystic winds. *Kalkipuranam* and *Skandapuranam* have been rendered as *Kilippattus* by Mr. Otuvil Sankarankutti Menon, that gifted blind bard of Ṭalappalli. His is an epic of endeavour and conquest over great obstacles. He is a brother of Otuvil Kunhi Krishna Menon whose *Kavimrgavali* created quite an unprecedented stir in the world of Malabar poets. There is an ease and grace in his poems which do not fail to charm those who read or hear them. The *Ramasvamedham* of Kāṭṭuḷḷil Achyuta Menon and the *Kilippattus* of Varavūr Śāmu Menon will not suffer in comparison with the great models of old days. The *Bhasha Puranams* of Vallathole and Pandit Vāsudēvan Mūssad also have successfully adopted the *Kilippattu* style.

There is a craze for Dravidian metres and a corresponding hostile attitude against rhyme and Sanskrit metres among a certain section of the Malayalam poets. This mentality among a few moderns is to be highly regretted, for a little thinking will show that there is no real substance, much less sufficient reason behind it.

Of the famous works of Kalidasa, Bhavabhuti, Sri Harsha, Bhasa, and Sudraka we have fine Malayalam renderings, and some of these are by those who have leanings for the Dravidian metres. Some Shakespearian dramas are also done into Malayalam. Mākōṭṭu Krishna Menon stood for Sanskrit culture. His renderings of *Chandakausikam* and *Lalitopakhyanam* deserve mention. C. Govindan Elayadam was an ideal Pandit of the old type who loved his pupils and was revered by them. He has invested his translations of *Tempest* and *Chandrahasa* with a simplicity and charm all his own. Kuṇḍūr Narayana Menon, was a compeer of Kodungallur Tampurans, Natuvom and Venmani Mahan. He has worked hard for the development of the Malayalam literature. His translations of *Malavikagnimitram*, *Meghadutu* and *Kumarasambhavam* are familiar to students of Malayalam. The artless piety and the simple diction of Natuvath Achchan's *Bhagavatdutu* have appealed to the masses to a very great degree.

Of *Mahakavyas* of the Sanskrit classic type we have a fair number. *Ramachandravilasam* of Padmanabha Kurup, *Kesaviyam* of Kesava Pillai, *Vanchisavamsam* and *Gosrisadityacharitam* and *Pandavodayam* of Kochunni Tampuran, *Rugmangadacharitam* of Pantalath Kerala Varma Tampuran, *Umakeralam* of Rao Sahib Uīlūr Parameswara Ayyar, *Chitrayogam* of Vallathole, *Sri Yesuvijayam* of K. Cheriyan Moppilay and *Rahguviravijayam* and *Raghavabhyudayam* of Mr. Vatakkankur Raja Raja Varma will arrest the attention of any scholar. Ullur is admittedly a profound scholar and a great poet. What is more : he works by day and by night to enrich the Malayalam language and its literature, in both of which he is acknowledged to be an authority. The late P. K. Narayana Pillai was also great as a scholar and poet, but his strenuous life as a lawyer and politician left him little leisure to bring forth as many works as his friend. His *Prasangatàrangani* and *Prayogadipika* sufficiently indicate his scholarship and his fine critical taste for literature. Vatakkankur Raja Raja Varma has, besides his two *Kavyas*, written a work called *Sahitisarvasvam*, a very useful book for advanced students and a history of the Sanskrit literature of Kerala. His *Sahitya Manjarì* contains a collection of his valuable essays on literary subjects. His style is free from verbal jugglery and enigmatic conceits. He is a good scholar and a fine poet. He is above all an enthusiast in the cause of the ordered progress of his mother-tongue. Kumāran Āśān has composed a number of fine poems on a variety of subjects. His *Fallen Flower*, *Nalini*, *Lila*, *Durawastha* and *Chandala Bhikshuki* are noteworthy for their style and suggestiveness. He was one of those honoured during the visit of His Royal Highness the Prince of Wales to Madras. Mr. Etamarath Victor's *Pazhaya Pana* and *Garland of Hymns* contain many elevating devotional songs. Mr. A. D. Hari Sarma, though a member of the Gauda-Saraswath community, is a fine student of Sanskrit and Malayalam, a fact that is amply borne out by his several prose and poetical works. But the one remarkable fact is the advent of Pandit K. P. Karuppan into the literary firmament of Malabar. He entered it with his *Balakalesam*, which secured the first prize in a competition instituted by a generous donor for the best drama fit to be staged at the completion of the sixtieth year of the penultimate Ruler of Cochin. I shall here transcribe a few lines from a Preface I wrote to that work at the time of its first publication in 1913. "Mr. Karuppan is a Valan, a boatman, by caste, a fact he is happily not ashamed of. But, if you expect to see in him an illiterate man tanned by the Indian sun, with a dirty bit of cloth round his head, armed with a paddle and seated at the helm of a country dug-out, you will be greatly disappointed. He is a fair young man, and dresses as decently as the reader himself. He is a good Sanskrit scholar and a poet of no mean order, and he deservedly occupies to-day the proud position of the Sanskrit Pandit of the Ernakulam Sirkar Girls' School. I should not be understood to have decried the calling of Mr. Karuppan's castemen. Certainly not; for his is as honourable, useful, and exciting a profession as that of any other community."

Balakalesam did not escape criticism and that of a virulent type. But the malicious attacks of a carping critic only produced, as its after-effect, a clearer sky for Mr. Karuppan and he rose in his official position and in the sympathetic estimation of the disinterested educated public of Malabar. The late Ruler of Cochin honoured him with the title of *Kavi-tilakan* and the University once appointed him as the Chairman of the Board of Examiners for its Oriental Titles Examination. Honours have not inflated his head nor made him proud. His rendering of *Bhaimiparinayam* and his *Lalitopaharam* and the numerous poems and musical dramas he has composed for School Day celebrations mark him out as one of the best poets of modern times. Speaking of musical dramas, the *Sadarama* of Kesava Pillai and the *Sangitanaishadham* of Mr. T. C. Achyuta Menon deserve special reference. Even illiterate coolies go about with snatches of songs from them in their mouths, so catching has been their melody. The number of clever poets and of prose-writers, males and females, who have risen and of others who are rising is legion. It is not possible in this short sketch to find space for them all. Using a lawyer's phrase, I can only submit that the names given are illustrative and not exhaustive. However, the name of Mr. G. Saunkara Kurup merits mention here not alone as the author of several poems but also as a clamant advocate of mystic poetry.

Another department of literature that is being cultivated is prose fiction. T. M. Appu Nedungadi's *Kundalatha* led the way. In form and finish it has reached a high level. But the novel that first attracted thousands of readers was Chandu Menon's *Indulekha.* It is a society novel and treats of the upper ten, their fashions and frivolities. There is a firmness in his handling his story. His racy diction and his graceful humour mark him out as the Thackeray of Malayalam literature. He has in his novel hit off certain characters with wonderful accuracy, and his Sūri Nambūri, Vythie Patter, Panchu Menon and others will live as long as our literature lasts to enliven passing hours.

Marthanda Varma of C. V. Raman Pillai has revivified a forgotten chapter of Travancore history. It enchains the attention of the reader from the first line to the last. There is life in his story, his persons and his dialogues. His characters have the variety, as they have the truth of history. It is one of the most brilliant things of its kind and will hold its own with any historical novel of any other country. He is also the author of several farces. Many novels have come to light in these years; originals and translations. Among these originals, the most recent is *Sakuntala Devi*, a two-volumed novel by Śrīmati Dēvaki Amma, a granddaughter of Chandu Menon, of which her forebear would have felt proud if he were alive to-day. Among translations, those of Śrīmati T. C. Kalyāṇi Amma deserve a reference here. For her literary works she was given the title of Sāhitya Sakhi by the late Ruler of Cochin. A. Narayana Puduval and E. V. Krishna Pillai are well-known as tellers of short stories.

History, biography, science, and critical studies are successfully trying to have their voices heard in Keralam. Malayalam can now boast of a few books on the first three subjects; while the beginnings of the last can be met with in the decent periodicals of the day.

To the making of the *History of Cochin* by the late K. P. Padmanabha Menon much patient research work has gone. Lives of many of the Malabar Men of Letters have been published recently. Though they lack the form and the finish of similar series in English, yet it has to be said to their credit that they have made a fair start. Except a few works by Christian Missionaries, which, from their quaint phraseology, are of little or no practical value at the present day, Dr. Krishnan Pandalay's translation of Sir H. Roscoe's Primer on Chemistry may be said to be an epoch-marking book. Others have followed him, notably Mr. M. Udaya Varma Raja with his *Introductory Primer* and Mr. M. Rajaraja Varma, with a primer on *Physical Geography*. The latter has written several other useful works on scientific and historical subjects. The want of a standard glossary of scientific terms stands in the way of the writing of useful manuals on scientific topics.

Many works in the range of Malayalam literature, notably the great epics, contain gems of philosophical thought, pure and serene. The several Malayalam renderings of the great Puranas, the brochure on *Advaita Philosophy* from the pen of H. H. Kerala Varma, the late learned Elaya Raja of Cochin, and the translations of the *Bhagavat Gita* by A. Govinda Pillai, Damodaran Kartha and T. V. Ananthan Nayar, will, I dare say, give a proper setting to the above so as to enhance their value and to induce Malayalees to venture to still higher levels in the search after the purest and the most precious jewel of all. The scholarly commentaries of the Bhagavat Gita in Malayalam by K. M. and Dr. L. A. Ravi Varma and also those of some of the Upanishads by the latter will contribute greatly to popularise the Advaita Philosophy among the educated Malayalees.

I would fail in a pleasing duty were I to omit the names of those who play the not very ambitious but by no means insignificant role of text-book writers. A. R. Rajaraja Varma, Kuppakātt Narayana Menon, M. Krishnan, Joseph Muliyil, Mr. Krishan Thampi, and others have written several useful books in Malayalam which are being taught in several schools in Malabar.

There are those who say that their official duties allow them little or no time to engage themselves in literary or scientific pursuits. Every one who has read anything of the life and work of the great politicians and professors of England and of other countries will know that this contention is only of a plausible nature. Even here, there are examples of those like A. R. Rajaraja Varma, A. Govinda Pillai, Mr. M. Rajaraja Varma, C. Achyuta Menon, Kundur Narayana Menon, Ullur, Pailo Paul, Krishnan Thampi, Mr. L. V. Ramaswami Ayyar and others to falsify this newlangled notion. Among these, the names of Mr. M. Rajaraja Varma, Professor Krishnan Thampi and Mr. L. V. Ramaswami Ayyar deserve special mention. They worked not for fame nor for money, but for the sole purpose of enriching Malayalam literature. Besides the renderings of *In Memoriam* and of Goldsmith's *Hermit*, and a commentary to Koil Thampuran's *Anyapadesam* and Rajaraja Varma's *Meghaduta*, the first has published several works in prose. The late Thampi is the author of several works in Sanskrit and in Malayalam, and always tried to introduce new forms of poetical literature into Malayalam. Mr. L. V. Ramaswami Ayyar is a linguist who, by his researches on the morphology of the Malayalam Language, has gained an international reputation.

PERIODICAL LITERATURE

Newspapers and Magazines have breathed fresh life into the literature of the land. They have introduced a large race of literary men to the public. By their well-timed and judicious criticism, they have arrested the growth of poisonous and ephemeral literature and facilitated the production of much of what is healthy and vigorous.

Many of the papers and magazines are conducted with honesty, devotion and ability, while a few exist more to parade the passions and prejudices of ill-advised partisans and to gain notoriety by constant appearance in law-courts than for the political, social or literary advancement of the country. It is indeed a matter for regret that journals of this class are on the increase which, no doubt, points to the prurient taste of a certain section of the reading public that stands very much in need of some drastic remedy. There are a number of daily and weekly newspapers conducted in Malayalam.

When speaking of newspapers, the one name that suggests itself to my mind is that of

Kunhi Raman Nayanār. He was the best Malayalam newspaper correspondent of his day. His chaste diction and his humour invest his writings with an indefinable charm. If only he had worked, he could have easily gained an undying name in the journalistic history of his country. He started *Kerala Sanchari*, a weekly. He used to style himself as Kesari. Some of his writings have been gathered together in the form of a book. Another able journalist was Ramakrishna Pillai. His wife Srīmaṭy T. B. Kalayāṇi Amma, who wields a facile pen, has written about her husband in her reminiscences called *Vyazhavatta Smaranakal*.

The first Malayalam Magazine was *Vidya Vilasini*. It made its name as the medium of publication of *Bhasha Sakunthalam*. It closed its career after a fitful life of a few years. Then came *Vidya Vinodini*, under Mr. C. Achyuta Menon. It soon became a power in the land. To gain a public audience even great poets availed themselves of *Vidya Vinodini*, while young writers of talent and genius served their apprenticeship under Mr. Menon. Mr. Achyuta

Menon is a great writer indeed. Wit and beauty, reason and grace, all are sweetly blended in his inimitable articles. His reviews of several works are real gems of prose.

Vidya Vinodini also had its day and ceased to be. Its place was filled up for a time by *Rasika Ranjini*, a monthly that was owned and conducted by H. H. Rama Varma Appan Tampuran of Cochin. It speaks volumes in favour of this prince that he, despising a life of learned leisure, should love to live laborious days for the benefit of his country and its literature. 'To write perfect prose' it has been rightly put 'is as difficult as to lead a perfect life.' His Highness is showing how to do both. His *Bhaskara Menon* and *Bhutarayan* are very good novels. His stray writings to journals are collected in four or five volumes called *Mangalamala*.

Bhasha Poshini is the name of the monthly conducted by the society of the same name. The late Varughese Mappillai, its first editor, was a man with a many-sided activity. He was a poet and the Secretary to an educational institution and to several societies and trading concerns. His capacity for taking pains was so wonderful that nothing produced by him or placed under him suffered for want of attention. His *Abraya Kutti* is a meritorious work. His contributions to periodical literature are marked by vigour and breadth of view. He was the life and soul of the *Bhasha Poshini Sabha*. In fine, he was a man with a heart to do good to his fellowmen ; and after his light and might he did it admirably well. Mr. M. Kumāran is the master of a melodious prose style effective to express every shade of feeling and of fine thoughts.

Kavanodayam, a journal published by the late Udaya Varma Raja of Kadathanad, was mainly devoted to the publication of poetical compositions. Udaya Varma (b. 1867 A. D.) maintained the high traditions of his ancient family. Himself a literary man he never failed to encourage men of letters.

There is an idea among certain persons in Cochin and Travancore that the output of literary works in British Malabar has not been commensurate with its extent and importance. This is an appropriate place I trust to enter my caveat against that wrong notion. The palaces of Kōlaṭṭiri, Kottayam Kōlikōte, Kōttakkal, Chirakal and Kōlathunād Rajas were centres of learning in ancient days, and sources of generous patronage to literature. Sukumara Kavi, the author of *Sri Krishna Vilasam* was a Malayali from North Malabar. *Krishnattam* and *Purva Bharatha Champu* are the works of Mānavēḍan Raja (1125 A. D.) of Calicut. And what of *Ramanattam*, popularly known as *Kathakali*? Veerakerala Varma (1665—1743), the originator of that and the author of eight dramatic pieces, was a Northerner; so too was his brother, Kerala Varma, the author of *Bhasha Valmiki Ramayanam* and of *Vairagya-Chandrodayam*. He helped Travancore during the Mogul invasion (1680—3). Cheruśśēri and Pūmṭānam, and Śankara Wārriar, who composed the *Sri Krishna Vijayam* in Sanskrit and *Pancharatnam* in Malayalam, were all from British Malabar. Mēppaṭṭūr Bhattaṭiri was a Northerner. Besides his famous Sanskrit works, he has written in Malayalam *Advaita Satakam*, *Chandrika Maholsavam*, *Kuttappathakam* and a number of *Champu-pra-*

bandhams. So also Kallekulamgara Raghava Pisharoti, the author of *Vetala Charitam, Panchatantram* and *Setumahatmyam*, hails from British Malabar. Kōlaṭṭiri Swarūpam had *Yogams* and *Sadassukal* for the encouragement of poets and the development of literature. Ravi Varma of Kolattiri composed *Udaya Varma Charitam*, and Rama Varma made *Bharata Samgraham*, and Kataṭṭanāt Appan Tampuran wrote *Sadratnamala. Kuchela Vrttam* of Kōttūr Nambiyār, *Gautama Charitam* of Olayattu Sankara Poduval, *Harichandra Charitam Tullal* of Kunhi Bappu, and *Nalacharitam Manipravalam* of Mātāyi Mānnan Gurukkal are well-known works. Vedic hymns were for the first time rendered into Malayalam by a Namputiri of Talipparambu, and the first translation of *Bhagavat Gita* was by Kunhappu Gurukkal, and of *Koran* by Māyankutti Hāji. It was a Namputiri from Etakkāt that wrote *Prasnamargam* ; *Bhaskaram*, a Malayalam commentary to *Ashtangahrdayam*, is by Uppōte Kaṇṇan ; and, about 200 years ago, Kerala Varma of Chirakkal Kovilakam wrote an annotation to *Ekadesam.*

Punnaśśēri Nampi, Seshagiri Prabhu, Muliyil Krishnan, V. C. Balakrishna Panikker, K. C. Narayanan Nampiyar, Kuttyappan Nampiyar, Mr. Unnikrishnan Nayar, Mr. Kuttamaṭṭ Kunhikrishna Kurup, Mr. Balakrishnan Nayar, Mr. P. S. Warriar, Mr. P. K. Warriar—each of them can be considered a host in himself. I can multiply instances. But I believe I have said enough to show that the contention is not just.

What Udaya Varma and his *Kavanodayam* did for Malayalam Literature will ever be recorded in its glorious history. He was assisted by Krishna Warriar, whose scholarship and poetical talents are seen in his *Bhasha Ramayana Champu.* The Raja is the author of *Rasikabhushanam*, *Priyadarsika* and *Kavitabharanam.*

Vyavahara Chintamani, a monthly devoted to law, and *Dhanvanthari*, one devoted to medicine, did very useful work. Another magazine that once came into prominence was *Sarada.* It was edited by three Nayar ladies and was intended for the instruction and amusement of the ladies of Malabar.

Lekshmibhai, another monthly that served the same purpose, has long been in the journalistic field. A few years ago, it celebrated its Silver Jubilee. To have lived to do it is itself a creditable feat. But when one remembers of the silent but solid service it has been doing for the popular education of the ladies of Malabar, one cannot but give it its meed of praise with a grateful heart. *Keralan,* that was edited by Mr. Attur Krishna Pisharoti, was a high-class magazine devoted to scholarly articles. It was in that that Mr. Raman Nambiyassan's brilliant romance *Keralesvaran* was first published. Mr. Krishna Pisharoti is an erudite scholar, and he has done yeoman service to Malayalam Literature by his scholarly editions of *Lilatilakam* and *Unninili Sandesam* and by his rendering of *Sakunthalam.* His articles on the Bhasa question, his booklets on the early history of Keralam and on the history of Malayalam Literature are all marked for their scholarship and research work. Of the new ventures the *All-Kerala Parishat Magazine* under the editorship of Ulloor, and *Sahrdaya* started under the guidance of V. Krishnan Tampi are expected to do substantial work in consolidation and research work and in the moulding of the future growth of our language and literature. The former is the organ of the *Samastha Kerala Sahitya Parishat*, a learned body which has secured the patronage of the Rulers of Cochin and Travancore.

Under the head of newspapers, there are at present several dailies and weeklies that are doing good work to promote the cause of the Malayalam language and literature. I should also here record the great service that has all along been rendered by respectable printing and book-selling firms to the growth of Malayalam literature.

MALAYALEES WHO HAVE WRITTEN IN ENGLISH.

To give at least an apparent completeness to this sketch, I think it is necessary to take a cursory view of the work done in English by the natives of this country. For 'the work of administration and of the Courts of Justice is more or less carried on in English, higher education is imparted in English, and English is the one language in which the people of the different provinces in India could at present communicate with one another'. But it does not fall within the purview of this sketch to speak of those Malayalees who have won a name as statesmen, as administrators, judges, lawyers, public speakers or educationists. I shall refer only to a few of those who have won fame by their published works.

P. Sankunni Menon's *History of Travancore* is a valuable work. But with much that is good one finds in it much of what is bad also. The writings of his son, K. P. Padmanabha Menon, are, however, free from this defect. His *History of Kerala* in four large volumes is marked by historical accuracy and by the logical rigour in its treatment, and is the outcome of a life-long study and of patient and persevering investigation. The late Judge K. G. Sesha Iyer, Seshagiri Prabhu, Balakrishnan Nayar, Mr. T. K. Gopala Panikkar, Mr. K. Rama Pishāroti, Mr. K. V. Krishna Iyer and Mr. Balakrishna Wārriar, like the late Menon, have worked at the rich, unexplored mines of the antiquities of Keralam. Prabhu was an enthusiast in his work and was, besides, a profound Sanskrit scholar. Many of the Census Reports of Cochin and Travancore are veritable storehouses of information concerning those States. They are very readable volumes and reflect great credit on the historical researches and literary ability of C. Achyuta Menon, M. Sankara Menon, Mr. T. K. Sankara Menon, N. Nagamiah and Drs. Subramania Ayyar and Kunjan Pillai. So too the Report of the *Jenmi-Kutiyan* Committee written by the late Judge Raman Thāmpi. But foremost among this band of workers stood the late Professor Sundaram Pillai. His *Sovereigns of Venad* is a substantial piece of work which would do credit to any antiquarian of any land. His services to the cause of historical literature deserve to be remembered with gratitude.

Nor are poets wanting in Malabar. *Firebrand*, evidently a political drama, shows that its author, T. Govinda Menon, was conversant with the subtleties of English prosody and that his mind was saturated with the best works of Shakespeare.

It is a matter for congratulation that at one time two of the four dailies of Madras were edited by Malayalees. The late G. Parameswaram Pillai, who ably edited the *Madras Standard*, has also written two books, *Representative Men of India* and *London and Paris*, which have won for him a European reputation. He was a self-made man. In spite of his poverty, G. P. Pillai worked himself up to the pinnacle of fame. The story of his life is worthy of being written, because of the lessons of patience and perseverance which it teaches to his countrymen, because of the originality of his thought and effort, and because his life exemplifies in an emphatic way that real worth will rise though by poverty depressed. C. Karunakara Menon was for a long time the Editor of the *Hindu*. The ability and earnestness he brought to bear on his work gained for his paper a wide circle of readers. K. Menon edited *The Madras Review* also. This review as well as the *Madras Law Journal* were originally started by the late Sir Sankaran Nayar who rose to be the Advocate-General of Madras, a High Court Judge and a member of H. E. the Viceroy's Executive Council. His writings and speeches were marked by sound common sense and manly vigour. *The Malabar Quarterly*

Review of C. V. Subramania Ayyar devoted itself to the discussion of topics relating to Malabar and was a first class magazine. U. Balakrishnan Ṅayar was another gifted writer of English prose.

I shall now close this somewhat desultory paper. I have spoken of the dim beginnings of Malayalam Literature, of the clouds that overcast it for a time and of the effulgence of brilliant constellations that followed the darkness. The future is with us. By arduous work and with patriotic zeal, it rests with the sons of Malabar to hasten the advent of a glorious future. We may in the meantime console ourselves with the encouraging thought that we are in the dawn of a great era and in that dawn to be alive is very heaven.

INDEX

A

B

C

D

E

F

G

G—(*cont.*)

H

I

J

K

K - (*cont.*)

L

M

N

O

P

R

R—(*cont.*)

S

T

T—(*cont.*)

U

V

Y